WE
HAVE HEARD
RAVENS

Poems drawn from
DOROTHY WORDSWORTH'S
Journals

CATHERINE SIMMONDS

FLAGON PRESS

First published 2008
by Flagon Press
Whitelackington
Ilminster

Introduction and notes
by Catherine Simmonds
All rights reserved
© Catherine Simmonds 2008

Cover painting © Alice Crane 2007

A CIP record for this book is available from the British Library

ISBN 978-0-9557073-4-6

This edition limited to 1000 copies
Designed by Andrew Crane
Typeset by Harry McIntosh of Speedspools, Edinburgh
in 10 pt Monotype Centaur roman and italic
Paper used for this edition is
text – supreme book wove 100gsm
cover – waterford rough 300gsm

Printed in Ilminster by Terry Wright, Rose Mills Print,
on Heidelberg original letterpress machines

This book is dedicated to

John Frederick George Mann

1911 – 2005

INTRODUCTION

Dorothy Wordsworth, whether she cared to acknowledge
it or not, wrote herself straight into the nerve-centre of
English Romanticism with the journals she kept during
her years as companion, champion, critic, and fiercely
loyal younger sister to the poet William Wordsworth.
'There is simply nothing like it anywhere else' writes
Pamela Woof of Dorothy's Grasmere journal, and most
readers who set out to examine Dorothy's extant journals
out of curiosity concerning her now famous literary
companions will have little to prepare them for the
immediacy and skill with which this young woman set
about recording her day to day life, and the powerful
perceptive responses she drew from the world around her.

She lived a very unusual life, which despite the financial
and emotional limitations arising from the early death of
both her parents, also provided unexpected freedoms,
one of which was the opportunity to live with her
brother and develop herself as a writer. Like William she
was a great walker and gladly walked considerable
distances both in company and alone. Journal writing
suited her sharply observant mind and eye. She loved the
fine detail of the natural world around her and although
she was moved both by the power and beauty of the
landscapes she experienced and the harsh circumstances
of the country people whose stories she wove into her
journals, she is marked out by her ability to record what
she sees clearly, without sentiment or embellishment.

That both Wordsworth and Coleridge responded with
delight to her writing and to her natural vivacity of mind
encouraged her. The great strides they all made together
as friends and writers from 1795 onwards, when at
Racedown Lodge in Dorset they first began sharing their

lives, poetry, favourite walks and observations, accelerated Dorothy's literary development – just as her responsive, lucid journals fed straight into the heart of the two mens' poetry. However, she also defined herself as a writer against these two men, whose poetry she admired so wholeheartedly, and always felt her own poetic gift to be inferior. From time to time flashes of upset and frustration break up through the clear surface of her writing.

Irrespective of her reservations about her gifts, her writing has never ceased to impress itself on new audiences with its quality and engagement. She was never one to shy away from taking risks with language and would alter and redraft key descriptive lines in her journal until she was satisfied they rang true.
The straightforward almost muscular nature of her writing means that her stylistic legacy strikes at us across the centuries – streamlined and wonderfully, curiously modern. 'We Have Heard Ravens' has been drawn up using less than 7000 of her words, a tiny fraction of her original output, and is intended as an experiment and a tribute to an extraordinary English writer who brought her whole self to bear not only upon her writing craft but upon her relationships with those close to her, and who left English literature immeasurably richer.

In this book some of Dorothy's journal spellings have been modernised to aid the reader.

C.T.S

THE ALFOXDEN JOURNAL

January 20th

The green paths
down the hillsides
are channels for streams.

The young wheat
is streaked
by silver lines of water.

After the wet dark days
the country seems more populous –
it peoples itself in the sunbeams.

The purple-starred hepatica
spreads itself in the sun.
The slanting woods –

the light through
their thin network
of upper boughs.

Upon the ridge
the shafts of the trees
show like the columns of a ruin.

January 23rd

Bright sunshine, went out at three, the sea perfectly calm
streaked with deeper colour, on our return a gloomy red.

The sun gone down, the crescent moon, Jupiter and Venus.
The sound of the sea distinctly heard on the tops of the hills.

We attribute this to the bareness of the trees, to the absence
of the singing of birds, the hum of insects, that noiseless noise

which lives in the summer air. The villages marked out
by beautiful beds of smoke. The turf fading into the mountain road.

The scarlet flowers of the moss.

January 25th

The sky spread over
with one continuous cloud

whitened by the light of the moon
which, though her dim shape was seen

did not throw forth so strong a light
as to chequer the earth with shadows.

At once the clouds seemed to cleave asunder
and left her in the centre of a black-blue vault.

She sailed along, followed by a multitude of stars
small and bright and sharp.

January 27th

Upon the whole an uninteresting evening.
The manufacturer's dog makes a strange uncouth howl.
It continues many minutes after there is no noise.
It howls at the murmur of the village stream.

January 29th

A very stormy day. William walked
to the top of the hill to see the sea.

Nothing distinguishable
but a heavy blackness.

An immense bough
riven from one of the firs.

Set forward to Stowey[1] at half past five.
A violent storm in the wood –
we sheltered under the hollies.

Left the wood when nothing remained
of the storm but the driving wind
and a few scattering drops of rain.

Presently all clear. Venus first
showing herself between the struggling clouds
afterwards Jupiter appeared.

The road to Holford glittered like a stream.
On our return, the wind high –
a violent storm of rain and hail at the Castle of Comfort.

All the heavens seemed in one perpetual motion
when the rain ceased, the moon appearing
now half veiled now retired behind heavy clouds –

the stars still moving, the roads very dirty.

1) Samuel Taylor Coleridge lived at Nether Stowey in Somerset and it was in order to be nearer to him that William and Dorothy, upon quitting their lodgings near Birdsmoorgate in West Dorset, had taken up the lease on Alfoxden House near Holford.

February 1st

Set forward towards Mr Bartelmy's.
The sun shone clear but all at once
a heavy blackness hung over the sea.

The trees almost roared
and the ground seemed in motion
with the multitudes of dancing leaves.

Still the asses pastured in quietness under the hollies
undisturbed by these forerunners of the storm.
The wind beat furiously against us as we returned.

Full moon. She rose in uncommon majesty over the sea
slowly ascending through the clouds.
Sat with the window open an hour in the moonlight.

February 2nd

Walked through the wood and onto the downs before dinner.
A warm pleasant air. The sun shone
but was often obscured by straggling clouds.

The redbreasts made a ceaseless song in the woods.
The wind rose very high in the evening.
The room smoked so we were obliged to quit it.

Young lambs in the coombe, thick legs, large heads
black staring eyes, gaunt as a new-dropped lamb.

February 3rd

A mild morning, the windows open.
Redbreasts singing in the garden.
Walked with Coleridge over the hills.
The sea at first obscured by a vapour
which slid in one mighty mass along the seashore.
The distant country purple in the clear dull air
overhung by straggling clouds that sailed over it.
I never saw such a union of earth, sky, and sea.
The clouds beneath our feet spread themselves to the water
and the clouds of the sky almost joined them.
Gathered sticks in the wood – a perfect stillness.
The redbreasts sang upon the leafless boughs.
Of a great number of sheep in the field only one standing.
The moonlight at nine, still, warm as a summer's night.

February 4th

Midges spinning in the sunshine.
The songs of the lark and redbreast.
Daisies upon the turf, catkins upon the hazels
honeysuckles budding, the furze gay with blossom.

The sheep have rubbed the moss from the palings
leaving locks of wool and the red marks
with which they are spotted
upon the wood.

February 5th

In the continued singing of birds
distinguished the notes of a blackbird or thrush.

The sea overshadowed by a thick dark mist
the land in sunshine.

The sheltered oaks and beeches
still retaining their brown leaves.

Observed some trees putting out red shoots –
What trees are they?

February 8th

Went up the park and over the tops of the hills.
Sat a considerable time upon the heath
its surface restless and glittering with the motion
of the scattered piles of withered grass
and the waving of the spider's threads.

On our return, mist still hanging over the sea
but the opposite coast clear, the rocky cliffs
distinguishable. As we stood on the sunless hill
we saw the hills of grass – light and glittering
and the insects passing.

February 22nd

Coleridge came in the morning to dinner.
William and I walked to the woodlands.

The moon and two planets;
sharp and frosty.

Met a razor grinder
with a soldier's jacket on.

The sea very black, making a noise – loud
as if disturbed, and the wind was silent.

February 24th

Brown fallows
the springing wheat
like a shade of green
over the brown earth.

A few wreaths of blue smoke
spreading along the ground.
The oaks and beeches in the hedges
retain their yellow leaves.

The far prospect on the land side
islanded with sunshine.
The sea like a basin
full to the margin.

March 21st

A quiet shower of snow
was in the air more than half our walk.

At our return the sky partially shaded with clouds.
Two night birds startled from the great elm.

The horned moon is set.

April 2nd

A very high wind.
Coleridge came to avoid the smoke
and stayed all night.

We walked in the wood.
The still trees only gently bowed their heads
as if listening to the wind.

The hollies in the thick wood
unshaken by the blast.
Only when it came

with greater force
was it shaken by the rain drops
falling from the bare oaks above.

April 15th

Set forward to Crookham
walked about the squire's grounds.
Quaint waterfalls where nature
was striving to make beautiful
what art had deformed.

Ruins, hermitages & c. & c.
In spite of all these things
the dell beautiful
through everywhere planted
with unnaturalised trees.

Happily we cannot shape the huge hills
or carve out the valleys according to our fancy.

THE GRASMERE JOURNAL

May 14th I

William and John set off into Yorkshire, cold pork in their pockets.
I sat a long time upon a stone at the margin of the lake.
After a flood of tears my heart was easier.

The lake looked to me dull and melancholy.
The weltering on the shores seemed a heavy sound.
The wood rich in flowers. The crab trees coming out.

Met a blind man driving a very large beautiful bull and cow –
he walked with two sticks. Came home by Clappersgate.

*2) William and Dorothy left Alfoxden in June 1798
and took up with Coleridge's plan to live and study in
Germany. Lyrical Ballads was published while they
were in Germany. On their return to England they
decided to return north to their native Cumbria. The
Grasmere Journal covers the first few years of their
time at Dove Cottage, although Dorothy's December
1800 to October 1801 journal never survived.*

May 14th II

A young woman begged at the door.
She had come on Sunday morn

from Manchester with two shillings
and a slip of paper

which she supposed a bank note.
It was a cheat.

She had buried her husband
and three children

within a year and a half
all in one grave

burying very dear
paupers all put in one place

twenty shillings paid
for as much ground

as will bury a man
a grave stone to be put over it

or the right will be lost.
11/6 each time the ground is opened.

May 16th

As I was going out in the morning
I met a half crazy old man.

He showed me a pincushion
and begged a pin.

He began in a kind of indistinct voice
in this manner:

'Matthew Jobson's lost a cow
Tom Nichol has two good horses strained

Jim Jones's cow's broken her horn.'
He went into Aggy's

persuaded her to give him some whey
and let him boil porridge.

She declares he ate two quarts.

May 27th

A very tall woman, tall much beyond
the measure of tall women, called at the door.

She had on a very long brown cloak, her face had plainly
once been fair. She led a little bare-footed child about two years old.

She said her husband who was a tinker was gone before
with the other children. I gave her a piece of bread.

Beside the bridge at Rydal I saw her husband
sitting by the road, two asses feeding;

two young children at play upon the grass.
The man did not beg. A quarter mile further

I saw two boys before me, one about ten
the other about eight years old chasing a butterfly.

They were wild figures not very ragged
but without shoes and stockings.

The hat of the elder was wreathed round with yellow flowers.
The younger, whose hat was only a rimless crown

had stuck it round with laurel leaves.
They continued at play till I drew very near.

Then they addressed me with the begging cant
and whining voice of sorrow.

I said I served your mother this morning.
Oh says the elder you could not serve our mother

for she's dead and my father's on at the next town
he's a potter. I persisted in my assertion

that I would give them nothing. Says the elder
Come lets away and away they flew like lightning.

I saw them go up to Matthew Harrison's house
creeping with a beggars complaining foot.

On my return through Ambleside
I met in the street the mother driving her asses.

In the two panniers were the two little children
whom she was chiding and threatening with a wand.

The woman had told me in the morning she was of Scotland
which her accent fully proved, but that she had lived at Wigton

that they could not keep a house
so they travelled.

May 28th

Walked up to the rocks above Jenny Dockeray's.
Sat a long time upon the grass –
the prospect divinely beautiful.

If I had three hundred pounds and could afford
to have a bad interest for my money I would buy that estate
and we would build a cottage there to end our days.

I went into the garden and got white and yellow lilies
and periwinkle, which I planted. Sat under the trees with my work.
A beautiful evening – the crescent moon above Helm Crag.

June 1st

I lay upon the steep of Loughrigg – my heart dissolved in what I saw.
I was not startled but recalled from my reverie by a noise
as of a child paddling without shoes.

I looked up and saw a lamb – it approached as if to examine me
and stood a long time. I did not move. At last it ran past me
bleating along the pathway.

I saw a hare on the high road.
The post has not come in.

Wednesday June 25th

A very rainy day –
I made a shoe.

In the evening
I went above the house

and gathered flowers
which I planted – foxglove & c.

Wednesday September 3rd

A fine coolish morning
I ironed till half past three.

I then went to a funeral
at John Dawsons.

About ten men and four women
bread and cheese and ale.

They talked sensibly
cheerfully about common things.

The dead person fifty-six years of age
buried by the parish.

The coffin neatly lettered, painted black
and covered with a decent cloth.

They set the corpse down at the door
and while we stood within the threshold

the men with their hats off
sang a verse of a funeral psalm.

There were no near kindred
no children.

When we got out of the dark house
the sun was shining.

The prospect looked so divinely beautiful
as I never saw it.

It seemed more sacred
yet more allied to human life.

The fields – neighbours
of the churchyard

were green as possible
with the brightness of the sunshine.

I thought she was going to a quiet spot
and could not help weeping very much.

September 14th

Made bread
a sore thumb from a cut
a lovely day
read Boswell
under the bright yellow leaves.

Saturday 11th October

The colours of the mountains soft and rich with orange fern.
The cattle pasturing upon the hilltops.

Kites sailing as in the sky above our heads.
Sheep bleating in lines and chains and patterns.

They come down and feed
on the little green islands in the beds of the torrents.

The sheep fold is falling away.
It is built nearly in the form of a heart

unequally divided.

Look down the brook and see the drops rise upwards
and sparkle in the air, at the little falls, the higher sparkles the tallest.

Friday November 7th

A cold rainy morning.
William still unwell.
The michaelmas daisy droops.
The pansies are full of flowers.
The ashes are green, all but one
but have lost many leaves.
The copses are quite brown.
The poor woman and child
from Whitehaven drank tea –
nothing warm that day.

Tuesday November 24th

John Green's house looked pretty under Silver How.
We were stopped at once – our favourite birch tree
yielding up to the gusty wind with all its tender twigs.

The sun shone upon it and it glanced in the wind
like a flying sunshiny shower. It was a tree in shape –
with stem and branches, but it was like a spirit of water.

The other birch trees near it looked bright and cheerful
but it was a creature by its own self among them.

Snow upon the ground thinly scattered.
It snowed after we got up
and then the sun shone
and it was very warm though frosty.

A woman came who was travelling with her husband.
'I was once an officer's wife I, as you see me now.
My first husband married me at Appleby.
I had eighteen pounds a year for teaching a school.

And because I had no fortune his father turned him out of doors.
I have been in the West Indies. I lost the use of this finger.
Just before he died he came to me and said
he must bid farewell to his dear children and me.

I had a muslin gown like yours.
I seized hold of his coat as he went from me
and slipped the joint of my finger.
He was shot directly.'

1 8 0 2

I found a strawberry blossom in a rock
the little slender flower had more courage
than the green leaves

for they were but half expanded
and the blossom was spread full out.
I uprooted it rashly

but felt as if I had committed an outrage
so I planted it again – it will have but a stormy life of it
but let it live if it can.

Monday February 8th I

The rain had been so cold that it hardly melted the snow.
We stopped at Park's to get some straw in William's shoes.
We walked on very wet through the cold clashy roads
in bad spirits at having to go as far as Rydal.

But before we had come again to the shore of the lake
we met our patient bow-bent friend with his little wooden box on his back.
'Where are you going?' said he. 'To Rydal for letters.'
'I have two for you in my box.' We lifted the lid and there they lay.

Poor fellow, he straddled and pushed on with all his might
but we soon outstripped him. I could not help comparing lots with him.
He goes at that slow pace every morning and having wrought a hard days work
returns at night, however weary he may be, takes it all quietly

and though perhaps he neither feels thankfulness nor pleasure
when he eats his supper and has no luxury to look forward to
but falling asleep in his bed, yet I daresay
he neither murmurs nor thinks it hard.

Monday February 8th II

The night was wild.
There was a strange mountain lightness
when we were at the top of White Moss.

I have observed it there in the evenings
being between two valleys
there is more of the sky there than any other place.

I have never felt such a cold night.
There was a strong wind. It froze very hard.
William left me with a little peat fire – it grew less.

I wrote on and was starved. I durst not go into the pantry
for fear of waking William. At two I went
and put my letters under Fletcher's door.

At first when I went to bed
I seemed to be warm, I suppose
because the cold air I had just left

no longer touched my body
but I soon found I was mistaken.
I could not sleep from sheer cold.

I had baked pies and bread in the morning.
Coleridge's letter contained prescriptions.

Tuesday February 9th

William had slept better.
He fell to work and made himself unwell.
We did not walk.

The funeral came by of a poor woman
who had drowned herself.
Some say she was hardly treated by her husband

others say he was a decent man
she an indifferent wife.
She had got up in the night and drowned herself in the pond.

I attempted a fable but my head ached
my bones were sore with the cold of the day before
and I was downright stupid.

Saturday March 13th

The hail stones looked clean and pretty
upon the dry clean road.

Little Peggy Simpson was standing at the door
catching the hail stones in her hand.

She grows very like her mother.
After tea I read to William –

that account of the little boys
belonging to the tall woman

and an unlucky thing it was
for he could not escape the very words

and so he could not write the poem.

I felt myself weak. William charged me not to go to Mrs Lloyds
but when he was gone I thought I would get the visit over
so I ate a beef-steak thinking it would strengthen me
so it did and I went off. Rydal vale was full of life and motion.

I went through the fields and sat half an hour afraid to pass a cow.
The cow looked at me and I looked at the cow and whenever I stirred
the cow gave over eating. On my return there was something in the air
that compelled me to serious thought. The hills were large, closed in by the sky.

As I climbed Moss the moon came out. Oh! the unutterable darkness of the sky
and the earth below the moon and the glorious brightness of the moon itself.
There was a vivid sparkling streak of light at this end of Rydal but the rest was very dark
and Loughrigg and Silver How were white and bright as if they were covered with hoar frost.

Once there was no moonlight to be seen but upon the island house.
I had many exquisite feelings when I saw this lowly building in the waters
among the dark and lofty hills with the bright soft light upon it.
It made me more than half I was tired a poet I was tired.[3]

3) *Dorothy jumbles her word order in her tiredness,*
meaning to say '– it made me more than half a poet'.
She goes on 'I was tired when I reached home I could
not sit down to reading and tried to write verses but
alas! I gave up expecting William and went soon to bed.
Fletcher's carts came home late.'

Tuesday March 23rd

A mild morning
William worked at the cuckoo poem
I sewed beside him.

After dinner he slept
I read German and at the closing of day
went to sit in the orchard.

He came to me
and walked backwards and forwards
we talked about Coleridge.

William repeated the poem to me
I left him there
and in twenty minutes he came in rather tired.

The fire flutters and the watch ticks
I hear nothing else
save the breathings of my beloved

and he now and then
pushes his book forward
and turns over a leaf.

The ground covered with snow.
The woman bought me a letter from William and Mary.[4]

It was a sharp and windy night.
Thomas Wilkinson came with me to Barton

and questioned me like a catechiser all the way.
Every question was like the snapping

of a little thread about my heart.
I was glad when he left me.

The moon travelled through the clouds
tingeing them yellow as she passed

with two stars near her, one larger than the other.
These stars grew or diminished

as they passed from or went into the clouds.
At this time William, as I found the next day

was riding by himself between Middleham
and Barnard Castle having parted from Mary.

4) *William had left on April 7th for the home of
Dorothy's childhood friend Mary Hutchinson to discuss
arrangements for their forthcoming wedding. His desire
to marry Mary was complicated by the fact that he
already had a young daughter in France, Anne Caroline
(b. 1792), by Annette Vallon. In order to settle this
situation Dorothy and William would travel to Calais
to meet with Caroline and Annette, with whom they
had maintained a correspondence despite the difficulties
of the political situation, England having been at war
with France since 1793.*

Tuesday 13th April

I had slept ill and was not well and obliged to go to bed.
After tea I walked along the lake side.

The air was becoming still
the lake was of a bright slate colour

sheep resting, all things quiet.
When I returned Jane met me –

William was come.
The surprise shot through me.

He looked well but was tired
and went soon to bed after a dish of tea.

Thursday 15th April

When we were in the woods
beyond Gowbarrow Park
we saw a few daffodils
close to the water side.

We fancied that the lake
had floated the seeds ashore
that the little colony
had so sprung up.

But as we went along
there were more
and yet more and at last
under the boughs of the trees

we saw there was a belt of them
the breadth of a country road.
I never saw daffodils
so beautiful.

They grew among the mossy stones
about and about them –
some rested their heads upon these stones
as on a pillow for weariness

and the rest tossed and reeled and danced
and seemed as if they verily laughed with the wind
that blew upon them over the lake
ever glancing, ever changing.

There was here and there a little knot
a few stragglers a few yards higher up
but they were so few as not to disturb the simplicity –
the unity and life of that one busy highway.

We rested again and again. The bays were stormy
and we heard the waves at different distances –
and in the middle like the sea. Rain came on.
Deer in Gowbarrow Park like to skeletons.[5]

Friday April 16th (Good Friday)

When I undrew my curtains in the morning
I was much affected by the beauty and the change.
The sun shone, the wind had passed away.
The river was very bright as it flowed into the lake.

After William had shaved we set forward.
We saw a fisherman in the flat meadow
he came towards us and threw his line
over the two arched bridge.

A sheep came plunging down the river
its fleece dropped a glittering shower from its belly.
Primroses by the roadside, pilewort that shone
like stars of gold in the sun.

There were hundreds of cattle in the vale.
We watched the crows become white as silver
as they flew in the sunshine
and when they went still further

they looked like shapes of water
passing over the green fields.

*5) Dorothy's haunting description of the daffodils
pre-dates William's poem 'I Wandered Lonely as a Cloud'
by two years.*

Saturday April 17th

A mild warm rain. We sat in the garden all morning.
William dug a little. I transplanted a honeysuckle.

The lake was still, the sheep on the island
reflected in the water.

We walked after tea by moonlight.
The village was beautiful.

Helm Crag we observed very distinct.
The hedge round Benson's field is bound together

by an interlacing of ash sticks
which made a chain of silver when we faced the moon.

This morning I saw a robin chasing a scarlet butterfly.

Thursday April 29th

We went to John's Grove
William lay and I lay in the trench under the fence
he with his eyes shut and listening to the waterfalls and the birds.

There was no one waterfall above another
it was a sound of waters in the air – the voice of air.
The lake was still, there was a boat out.

Silver How reflected with purplish and yellow hues.
I observed the glittering silver line on the ridges of the backs of the sheep
which made them look beautiful but with something of strangeness

like animals of another kind
as if belonging to a more splendid world.

Saturday May 1st

As soon as breakfast was over we went into the garden and sowed scarlet beans.
I sowed the flowers. William helped me.

When the sun had got low enough we went to the Rock shade.
Two ravens flew high in the sky.

The sun shone on their belly and wings long after there was none of his light to be seen.
The landscape was fading, sheep and lambs quiet among the rocks.

Three solitary stars in the middle of the blue vault, one or two on the points of the high hills.
Heard the cuckoo today this first of May.

Tuesday May 4th

It is a glorious wild solitude under that lofty purple crag.
Its own self and its shadow below – one mass – all else was sunshine.

A bird at the top of the crag was flying round and round
and looked in thinness and transparency, shape and motion like a moth.

On the Rays we met a woman with two little girls, one in her arms
the other about four years old walking by her side –

a pretty little thing but half starved. She had on a pair of slippers
that had belonged to some gentleman's child, down at the heels.

It was not easy to keep them on but she walked carefully with them.
The mother told us her husband had left her, gone off with another woman

and how she 'pursued' them. Her fury kindled and her eyes rolled about
she changed again to tears. She was a Cockermouth woman, thirty years of age –

a child at Cockermouth⁶ when I was. I gave her a shilling.
We had the crescent moon with the 'auld moon in her arms'.

6) *Dorothy Wordsworth had been born at
Cockermouth, Cumbria on Dec 25th 1771. Her
mother died when she was six years old and although
her brothers remained in the care of their father until
his death in 1783, Dorothy was taken by relatives to
live in Yorkshire, later Penrith, then Norfolk. She never
attended her father's funeral. Her early separation from
her family grieved her deeply and made her determined
to rejoin her brothers in adulthood.*

We are sitting upon a seat
under the wall
which I found my brother building up
when I came to him
with his apple.

The small birds are singing
cuckoo calling
the thrush sings by fits
Thomas Ashburner's axe
is going quietly (without passion).

Hens are cackling, flies humming
the women talking together at their doors
plum and pear trees are in blossom
apple trees greenish
the crows are cawing.

We have heard ravens.
The ash trees are in blossom.
The stitchwort is coming out.
Celandine, violets and woodsorrel for ever more.
Little geranium and pansies on the wall.

The moon was a perfect boat –
a silver boat when we were out in the evening.
The birch tree is all over green
in small leaf, more light and elegant
than when it is full out.

It bends to the breezes as if for the love
of its own delightful motion.
Sloe thorns and hawthorns in the hedges.

Wednesday May 12th

We brought some heckberry blossom, crab blossom
the anemone nemrosa, marsh marigold, speedwell.
Anemones are in abundance and still the dear dear primroses;
violets in beds; pansies in abundance and the little celandine.

I pulled a branch of a taller celandine. Butterflies of all colours –
I often see some small ones of a pale purple lilac or Emperor's eye colour
something of the colour of the large geranium which grows by the lake side.
William pulled ivy with beautiful berries – I put it over the chimney piece.

Friday May 14th

Hail and snow showers all day. We went intending to get plants
and to go along the shore of the lake but there was no pleasure
in that difficult sauntering road in this ungenial weather.

I sat a while upon my last summer's seat –
the mossy stone, William's unemployed beside me
and the space between where Coleridge has so often lain.

The blue hyacinth is not quite full blown.
Gowans are coming out, marsh marigolds in full glory –
the little star plant, a star without a flower.

William tired himself with hammering at a passage.
I was out of spirits. After dinner he was better and I grew better.
We sat in the orchard – the sky cloudy, the air sweet and cool.

The young bullfinches in their partly coloured raiment
bustle about among the blossoms and poise themselves
like wire dancers or tumblers, shaking the twigs and dashing off the blossoms.

There is yet one primrose in the orchard, the stitchwort is fading
the vetches are blossoming and seeding
the wild columbines are coming into beauty.

In the garden we have lilies and many other flowers.
The scarlet beans are up in crowds. It has rained sweetly
for two hours and a half – the air is very mild.

The heckberry blossoms are dropping off fast, almost gone.
Barberries are in beauty, snowballs coming forward
May roses are blossoming.

Wednesday June 2nd

Yesterday an old man called –
a grey headed man, above 70 years of age.

He said he had been a soldier, that his wife
and children had died in Jamaica.

He had a beggar's wallet over his shoulders
a coat of shreds and patches altogether of a drab colour.

He was tall and though his body was bent
he had the look of one used to have been upright.

I talked a while to him and then gave him a piece of cold bacon
and a penny. Said he 'You're a fine woman.'

I could not help smiling. I suppose he meant
'You're a kind woman.'

Wednesday 2nd June

All the young oak trees are dry as powder.
A cold south wind portending rain.

We sat in deep silence at the window
I on a chair and William with his hand on my shoulder.

We were deep in silence and love a blessed hour.
On Tuesday evening we walked upon the turf near John's Grove.

The clouds of the western sky reflected a saffron light
upon the upper end of the lake.

All was still. We went to look at Rydal.
There was an alpine fire-like red upon the tops of the mountains.

We saw the lake in a new and most beautiful point of view
between two little rocks behind a small ridge that had concealed it from us.

The White Moss – a place made for all kinds
of beautiful works of art and nature.

Tuesday June 8th

Ellen and I rode to Windermere.
A fine sunny day neither hot nor cold.

We went out to the island, walked round it
and crossed the lake with our horse in the Ferry.

The shrubs have been cut away in some parts of the island.
I observed to the boatman that I did not think it improved.

He replied – 'We think it is, for one could hardly see the house before.'
It seems to me to be however no better than it was.

They have made no natural glades, it is merely a lawn
with a few miserable young trees standing as if they were half starved.

It is neither one thing or another – neither natural
nor wholly cultivated and artificial; and that great house –

Mercy upon us! If it could be concealed it would be well for all
who are not pained to see the pleasantest of earthly spots deformed by man.

But it cannot be covered. Even the tallest
of our old oak trees would not reach to the top of it.

The laburnums blossom freely on the island and in the shrubberies
on the shore – they are blighted everywhere else.

Roses of various sorts were out. The brooms were in full glory everywhere
'veins of gold' among the copses. The hawthorns in the valley fading away

beautiful upon the hills.

Wednesday June 9th

William slept ill.
A soaking all day rain.
The hawthorns on the mountain side
like orchards in blossom.
Brought rhubarb down.
It rained hard.
Ambleside fair.

Tuesday June 15th

The swallows come to the sitting-room window
as if wishing to build
but I am afraid they will not have the courage for it
but I believe they will build at my window.

They twitter and make a bustle and a little cheerful song
hanging against the panes of glass
with their soft white bellies close to the glass
and their forked fishlike tails.

They swim round and round and again they come.

Sunday 20th [7]

After tea we walked upon our own path for a long time.
We talked sweetly together about the disposal of our riches.
We lay upon the sloping turf. Earth and sky were so lovely
that they melted our very hearts.

The sky to the north was of a chastened
yet rich yellow fading into pale blue and streaked
and scattered over with steady islands of purple
melting away into shades of pink.

It made my heart almost feel like a vision to me.

7) *When William and Dorothy's father died*
unexpectedly in 1783 he was owed £4500 in salary
by Sir James Lowther. A lawsuit followed on behalf of
the Wordsworth children to recover the money but was
unsuccessful. In 1802 Lowther died and was succeeded
by his cousin who settled this long standing debt, along
with interest.

Friday July 9th[8]

The horse is come
Friday morning
so I must give over.

William is eating his broth
– I must prepare to go –
The swallows I must leave them

the well the garden the roses all –
Dear creatures
they sang last night

after I was in bed –
seemed to be singing to one another
just before they settled

Well I must go – farewell. – – –

8) *Dorothy and William were away from Dove
Cottage from July to October 1802, travelling via
Yorkshire and London to Calais to see Annette and
Caroline, then returning via Brompton, Yorkshire, where
the marriage of William to Mary Hutchinson takes
place. Mary returns with them to Dove Cottage in
October.*

Saturday July 31st [9]

We left London on Saturday. The city –
St Pauls with the river and a multitude
of little boats made a most beautiful sight
as we crossed Westminster bridge.
The houses were not overhung by their cloud of smoke
they were spread out endlessly yet the sun shone so brightly
with such a pure light that there was even something
like the purity of one of nature's own grand spectacles.
Still, as we went along the country was beautiful – hilly
with cottages lurking under the hills and their little plots
of hop ground like vineyards. It was a bad hop year –
A woman on the top of the coach said to me
'It is a sad thing for the poor people
for the hop-gathering is the woman's harvest.'

9) *Dorothy's description of St Paul's seen from*
Westminster bridge is clearly related to William's
'Sonnet Composed upon Westminster Bridge' although
because of a confusion over composition dates it is not
known which preceded which.

CALAIS I [10]

We walked by the sea-shore almost every evening with Annette and Caroline
or William and I alone. I had a bad cold and could not bathe at first but William did.

It was a pretty sight as we walked upon the sands when the tide was low
perhaps a hundred people bathing a quarter mile distant from us.

We had delightful walks after the heat of the day was passed
seeing far off in the west the coast of England like a cloud crested with Dover Castle.

As twilight came on, the fort at the entrance of the harbour of Calais
seemed to be reared upon pillars of ebony

between which the sea was seen in the most beautiful colours that can be conceived.
Nothing in romance was ever half so beautiful.

As the evening star sank down and the colours of the west faded away
the two lights of England came in view.

10) *Dorothy and William meet with Annette and
Caroline in Calais to make a settlement upon them
which will release William to marry Mary Hutchinson.*

CALAIS II[11]

One night I shall never forget.
The day had been very hot
William and I walked alone together on the pier.

The sea was gloomy for there was a blackness over all the sky
except when it was overspread with lightning
which often revealed to us a distant vessel.

Near us the waves roared and broke against the pier
and as they broke and as they travelled towards us
they were interfused with greenish fiery light.

It was also beautiful on the calm hot nights
to see the little boats row out of the harbour
with wings of fire and the sail boats with their fiery track

which they cut as they go along
and which close up after them with a hundred thousand sparkles –
Caroline was delighted – their streams of glowworm light.

11) *Dorothy's delight in the 'glowworm light' on the
channel recalls William surprising her at their Dorset
home with a real glow worm which he had carefully
carried back to show her. His 1802 poem 'Among All
Lovely Things My Love Had Been' recalls the incident
and describes how she 'Had noted well the stars, all
flowers that grew | About her home . . .' – perhaps a
reference to an earlier Dorset journal that has not
survived.*

GALLOW HILL

My Brother William
was married to Mary Hutcheson.

I slept a good deal of the night before and rose
fresh and well in the morning.

William had parted from me upstairs
I gave him the wedding ring with how deep a blessing.

I kept myself as quiet as I could
but when I saw the two men running up the walk –

coming to tell us it was over
I could stand it no longer and threw myself on the bed

where I lay in stillness, neither hearing or seeing anything.

Tuesday 5th October

We had a sweet ride until we came to a public house on the side of a hill.
We walked down to see the waterfalls. The sun was not yet set
the woods and fields were spread over with the yellow light of evening
which made their greenness a thousand times more green.
There was too much water in the river for the beauty of the falls
and even the banks were less interesting than in winter.
Nature had entirely got the better in her struggles against the giants
who first cast the mould of these works. One could not help feeling
as if there had been the agency of some mortal instruments
which nature had been struggling against without making a perfect conquest.
There was something so wild and new in this feeling – that God alone
has laid his hand upon it that I could not help regretting the want of it;
besides it is a pleasure to a real lover of nature to give winter all the glory he can
for summer will make its own way and speak its own praises.

Wednesday October 6th

Arrived at Grasmere 6 o'clock
Wednesday evening.

I cannot describe what I felt
and our dear Mary's feelings would –

I dare say not be easy to speak of.
We went by candle-light into the garden

and were astonished at the growth
of the brooms, Portugal laurels & c & c –.

Monday October 11th

A beautiful day.
We walked to the Easedale hills
to hunt waterfalls.

William and Mary left me
sitting on a stone
and went to Easedale Tarn.

I grew chilly
and followed them.

This approach to the Tarn is very beautiful.
We expected to have found Coleridge at home
but he did not come until after dinner.

He was well
but did not look so.

Monday October 31st

Mary and I walked to the top of the hill and looked at Rydal.
I was much affected when I stood upon the second bar of Sara's Gate.
The lake was perfectly still, the sun shone on hill and vale
the distant birch trees looked like large golden flowers –

nothing else in colour was distinct and separate
but all the beautiful colours seemed to be melted into one another
and joined together in one mass so that there were no differences
though an endless variety when one tried to find it out.

Monday November 8th

A beautiful day. William got to work again
and so continued all the morning, though the day
was so delightful that it made my heart linger
to be out of doors and see and feel
the beauty of autumn in freedom.

The trees on the opposite side of the lake
are of a yellow brown but there are one or two trees
opposite our windows (an ash tree for instance)
quite green as in spring. The fields are of their winter colour
but the island is as green as ever it was.

Friday December 24th

It was not an unpleasant morning to the feelings –
far from it. The sun shone now and then
and there was no wind.

But all things looked cheerless and distinct –
no meltings of sky into mountains. The mountains like stonework
wrought up with huge hammers.

Birthday

It is today Christmas day
Saturday 25th December 1802
I am 31 years of age.
It is a dull frosty day.

Tuesday January 11th 1803 I

Again I have neglected to write my journal
New Years Day is passed Old Christmas day
and I have recorded nothing.

On Christmas day I dressed myself
ready to go to Keswick in a returned chaise
but did not go.

On Thursday 30th December
I went to Keswick.
William rode before me to the foot of the hill.

We stopped close to the ledge
opposite a tuft of primroses
three flowers in full blossom

and a bud. They reared themselves up
among the green moss.
We debated long and hard

whether we should pluck them
and at last left them
to live out their day

which I was right glad of on my return
for there they remained
uninjured either by cold or wet.

A very cold day. William promised me he would rise
as soon as I had carried him his breakfast
but he lay in bed between twelve and one.

We talked of walking but the blackness of the cold
made us slow to put forward and we did not walk at all.
Mary read the prologue to Chaucer's tales to me.

William was working on his poem to Coleridge.
Since tea William has been working beside me
and here ends this imperfect summary.

I will take a nice Calais Book and will for the future
write regularly and, if I can, legibly. So much for this
my resolution on Tuesday night, January 11th 1803.

Now I am going to take tapioca for my supper
and Mary an egg, William some cold mutton –
his poor chest is tired.

ACKNOWLEDGEMENTS

I would like to acknowledge the encouragement, advice
and support of James Crowden, Harriet Thistlethwaite,
Gini Astley, Justin Orwin and Rick Smith, without whom
this project might have fallen by the wayside, as well as the
creative and professional input of Andrew Crane, Alice Crane
and Terry Wright. Thanks go to my parents in whose
garden I began this.

C.T.S